BRITISH BUS GARAGES
A PORTRAIT

MIKE RHODES

AMBERLEY

First published 2020

Amberley Publishing
The Hill, Stroud
Gloucestershire, GL5 4EP

www.amberley-books.com

Copyright © Mike Rhodes, 2020

The right of Mike Rhodes to be identified as
the Author of this work has been asserted in
accordance with the Copyrights, Designs and
Patents Act 1988.

ISBN 978 1 3981 0036 7 (print)
ISBN 978 1 3981 0037 4 (ebook)

British Library Cataloguing in Publication Data.
A catalogue record for this book is available from
the British Library.

Typesetting by Aura Technology and Software
Services, India. Printed in the UK.

Introduction

Commonly referred to as 'depots' or 'garages', with the former the preferred nomenclature for buildings which were designed to house trams or trolleybuses, such establishments first began to appear in the mid-to-late 1870s. These early tram depots were built to house horse-drawn tramcars and usually had outbuildings or stables attached for the comfort of the horses. The largest horse-drawn tramway systems were situated in Birmingham (several companies), Liverpool (Liverpool Tramways Company) and Manchester (Manchester & Salford Tramways Company). Each of these conurbations was home to a significant number of tram depots. The following decade brought the introduction of steam tramways, whereby the tramcars were hauled by specially designed steam engines which largely comprised an enclosed boiler and cab. These systems were especially prevalent in the industrial areas of the north-west and the Black Country where the supply of coal was plentiful.

In these early years the various local authorities had not been permitted to operate the tram systems themselves and they were usually leased to operating companies for a period of twenty-one years, as permitted under the Tramways Act of 1870. However, following the Light Railway Act of 1896, the restrictions on local councils were lifted and many local authorities sought to terminate the agreements and applied for Acts of Parliament to construct their own electric tramway systems. These invariably specified the construction of a completely new tram depot which quite often incorporated its own electricity generating station. While many of the horse and steam tram depot sites were unsuitable for the new works, some sites were substantially redeveloped with new depots. Four examples of these, which were still functioning in 2019, were Burnley Queensgate, which was first occupied by the Burnley & District Tramways Company in 1881, Blackburn Intact, which was originally home to the steam trams of the Blackburn, and Over Darwen Tramways Company and Clapton and Thornton Heath former London Transport garages, which were first occupied by horse tram depots belonging to the North Metropolitan Tramways Company (1882) and the Croydon Tramways Company (1881), respectively.

The span of the electric tram era, as a popular mode of transport, could probably be defined as from the end of the nineteenth century through to the early 1930s. During this period in excess of 300 tram depots were built. These ranged in size from Rochdale Corporation's small Britannia depot near Bacup, with a capacity for just two trams, through to what was claimed to be the largest tram depot in the country, namely New Cross in London, with a capacity for 280 cars. Both Glasgow and Birmingham, two of the largest systems outside of London, could boast over thirty-five tram depots between them. Even Aberdeen, Bradford, Bristol, Leeds and Sheffield had around a half a dozen or more car sheds apiece. The electric tram craze had progressed at such a rapid pace that (not surprisingly) both the trams and the permanent way became life expired over a short period of time. This presented the operators with a dilemma and most decided to abandon the trams and replace them with motorbuses or, in a number of instances, trolleybuses.

Early models of motorbuses became available towards the end of the first decade of the twentieth century and a number of bus garages were built which were generally modest affairs. As the design of the motorbus progressed more operators started up and a significant number of bus garages were built during the 1920s and 1930s. Established tramway operators built up fleets of buses and constructed purpose-built garages alongside the tramway facilities to service and maintain their bus fleets. Such operators included the Corporation Transport Departments of Birmingham, Blackpool, Bolton, Colne, Coventry, Nottingham, Rochdale, Salford and Southampton. At the same time tram depots throughout the country were converted for use by motorbuses. These included, among others, the municipal operations of Accrington, Ashton-under-Lyne, Birkenhead, Blackburn, Brighton, Burnley, Chester, Great Yarmouth, Grimsby, Hartlepool, Huddersfield, Leicester, Lytham St Annes, Newport, Northampton, Plymouth, Preston, Portsmouth, Reading, St Helens, Wallasey and Wolverhampton.

Not surprisingly the Second World War interrupted the plans of many operators. The abandonment of several tramway systems was delayed, and trams continued running in a number of towns and cities into the 1950s with the last system to be closed being that in Glasgow, on 31 August 1962 (Blackpool excepted). Edinburgh, Leeds and Sheffield opted for a policy of building completely new bus garages during the 1950s/early 1960s. While Liverpool opened new garages at Gillmoss and Speke, all its former tram depots were retained and converted for use by motorbuses. Similarly, Manchester Corporation's three initial large tram depots were converted into bus sheds and two of these, Hyde Road and Queens Road, were still functioning at the time of writing. At least two tramway systems were abandoned as a result of severe bomb damage during air raids – Coventry in November 1940 and Bristol in April 1941. In the case of the former a large bus garage had already been established in Harnall Lane which actually connected through to Priestly Bridge tram depot. Subsequently the whole of the Coventry Corporation bus fleet, which in the early 1950s amounted to some 280 buses, was based at this one garage until an additional garage at Sandy Lane was opened in 1954.

Some depots and garages were more than just a place to stable trams or park buses, they were architectural gems. Eastbourne Corporation's bus garage in Churchdale Road, Leicester Corporation's Abbey Park Road and Salford Corporation's Frederick Road tram/bus depots were all buildings to be admired and, alas, all three have been consigned to history and you would never have known that they had ever existed if it wasn't for historical photographs. Some depot sites have an intriguing history attached to them. For instance, in 1927 Ribble Motor Services opened a bus garage in Morecambe, which was located at the junction of Lancaster Road and South Avenue. The exact same location had previously been occupied by the Lancaster & District Tramways Company's horse-tram depot between 1890 and 1921. A visitor to the site in 2019 would find nothing more exciting than a supermarket store occupying this historical site.

Another depot site steeped in history is First Bus' King Street establishment in Aberdeen. The site was originally the home of the barracks of the Royal Aberdeenshire Highlanders from 1862 to 1914. In the latter year Aberdeen Corporation commenced construction of a tram depot on part of what had been the parade ground. Due to the outbreak of the First World War it was not brought into use until 1919. Not content with acquiring land from the army, the depot site was extended in 1932 with the acquisition of the adjacent Advocates Park Football Ground. Maidstone & District opened a new garage in Dartford in 1927; it was located in Priory Road and, as the name suggests, was built on land which had previously belonged to an ancient Priory. Indeed, some of the priory walls have remained in place to this day. The garage was taken over by the London Passenger Transport Board in 1933 and ended its days as a state-owned London Country bus garage. The site is now occupied by a DIY superstore.

Before the era of the private motorcar, tram and bus operators frequently provided what were referred to as 'Football Specials' to transport large numbers of supporters to the match. There are quite a few instances where tram depots/bus garages and football stadiums have been built very close to each other. Both Villa Park and St Andrew's, in Birmingham, originally had tramway depots for company; the former was close to Witton, while the latter was literally facing Coventry Road. In the old days, spectators at Halifax Town's Shay ground could actually stand on the embankment behind one of the goals which was in the shadow of Skircoat Road garage yard. This practice was witnessed by the author when 19,965 spectators were crammed into the ground on 31 July 1971 to see Town defeat Manchester United – Best, Charlton, Law et al. – two goals to one in the short-lived Watney Cup pre-season tournament. Southend United's Roots Hall ground rubbed shoulders with Eastern National's Prittlewell bus garage, while visitors to Portman Road in Ipswich could view the contents of the Corporation's Constantine Road bus garage before a match. Blackpool's Bloomfield Road ground was literally only separated from Rigby Road bus and tram depot by the width of several railway tracks which led into Central Station. Other football stadiums which had depots on their doorstep included Belle Vue (Doncaster Rovers), Deepdale (Preston North End), Home Park (Plymouth Argyle), Goldstone Ground (Brighton & Hove Albion), Ibrox (Glasgow Rangers), Ninian Park (Cardiff) and The Racecourse Ground (Wrexham). In at least three instances football stadiums and bus garages, which were built close together, have now both vanished from the landscape; Roker Park and Fulwell tram/bus depot in Sunderland, West Ham's Boleyn ground and Upton Park bus garage in London and Maine Road and Princess Road tram/bus depot in Manchester.

At least three garages have attained listed building status. Stockwell bus garage in London was opened in April 1952 and has a somewhat unusual concrete arch roof structure; it received Grade II listed status in 1988. Another garage which no longer functions as a bus depot, but which is a listed building, is Kingsway in Lancaster. Opened by Lancaster Corporation in July 1937, the building was retained by the council following the sale of the bus company to Stagecoach in August 1993. After several years of stagnation, a new residential development, ironically known as 'The Old Bus Depot', was finally opened in September 2009 and has incorporated the former bus garage building. The former administration block of Glasgow Corporation's Knightswood bus garage is also a listed building. Although the main garage buildings have been demolished and the site redeveloped, the admin block has been sympathetically incorporated into a new residential development.

In the UK the layout of virtually all bus garages was confined to a single level. The only exceptions that the author is aware of are Eastern Scottish's New Street garage in Edinburgh (opened in 1928) and London Transport's Victoria garage in Gillingham Street (opened in 1940). Whereas access was on the level both of these establishments had a basement area. Only the latter was still in existence in 2019 with the former having been closed during the 1990s and the building subsequently demolished. Another depot complex which could be considered to be on two levels was the combined Brightmet Street and Shiffnall Street tram depots in Bolton. Although housed in one building, these were considered to be two separate depots due to the difference in the levels between them; each had its own separate tramcar entrances.

What became the BET (British Electric Traction Company) and state-owned (Transport Holding Company) bus companies such as Bristol Omnibus, Crosville, Eastern Counties, Lincolnshire, Midland Red, Red & White, Ribble Motors, Southdown, Western National and Yorkshire Traction, to name but a few, all had networks of bus garages located throughout their operating areas. In terms of the number of garages or outstations used, Crosville probably tops the list at around sixty establishments, which were scattered throughout Cheshire, Merseyside and North and Central Wales. At its height Ribble was approaching thirty main garages and a number of small outstations in Cumbria and North Lancashire, each of which would be home to just a handful of buses. Ribble also had its own Central Repair Workshops in Preston, which was an entirely separate building complex from the main running sheds. Similarly, Bristol Omnibus (originally Bristol Tramways) had a major overhaul works at Brislington and Midland Red (BMMO) built its own buses for many years at its Carlyle Road works in Birmingham. During the tramway era the Corporations of Glasgow, Liverpool, Manchester and Southampton all had separate car overhaul/ construction works sited at Coplawhill, Edge Lane, Hyde Road and Portswood respectively.

The deregulation of bus services in October 1986 had a huge impact on the way bus operators now manage their fleets. Following privatisation, the majority of both municipal and former National Bus Company fleets (which were split up into smaller units) were eventually acquired by what today are a handful of major established bus operators. Many of the former garages are now but a distant memory and even those sites which still continue to function have been radically altered. Long gone are most of the individual brick and steel-clad buildings, which were erected by a myriad of long-established bus operators, and in their place have been erected soulless but functional basic-construction servicing and maintenance facilities which are, in the main, accompanied by large open-air parking lots. This approach has not always been the case as there are instances of the big group companies continuing to use original tram/bus depot buildings. These include Stagecoach's depots in Bedford (1913), Cheltenham (1901), Grimsby (1925) and Hastings (1905) and First Bus' use of the former Corporation tram depot in Great Yarmouth (1902).

The London Transport Executive was once responsible for over a hundred depots within its central and country areas. There is now a mixture of former London Transport garages and newly established operating centres. Following privatisation, a number of well-established garages with long histories were closed and razed to the ground. These included Edmonton, Hanwell, Kingston, Peckham, Southall, Upton Park, Walthamstow and West Ham, while Norwood, Poplar and Stonebridge Park remain standing but are no longer in use as bus garages. On the plus side Cricklewood garage was completely rebuilt in 2010 and a new state-of-the-art garage, which was widely acclaimed by the industry at the time, was opened in West Ham in 2009. A remarkable statistic, which was true in 2019, was that eleven of the still functioning London bus garages had accumulated 1,253 years of operation between them since opening as tram depots during the first decade of the twentieth century.

The garages and depots featured in this portrait are considered to be a representative selection across the wide spectrum of bus operation, from the large municipal and NBC bus fleets to the smaller independents. Many are depicted before deregulation and have generally been chosen to make the reader aware of just how the industry has changed over recent decades, and how many former bus and tram depots no longer form part of Britain's architectural landscape. It has been a fascinating journey in carrying out the research for this work and the reader is directed to the 'oldmapsonline' website, from which the location and layout details of virtually all the original tram depots can be ascertained from copies of the very detailed early ordnance survey maps. The author would also like to acknowledge reference made to the book *London Transport Bus Garages Since 1948* by J. Joyce. All the photographs contained in this book were taken by the author, who retains copyright.

Mike Rhodes
February 2020

Ribble Motors had over twenty main garages scattered about its vast operating area. However, none was more unusual than Lord Street in Southport. The building was originally a railway station opened by the Southport & Cheshire Lines Extension Railway on 1 September 1884. It was closed by BR on 7 January 1952 and reopened by Ribble as a combined garage and bus station on 28 June 1954. Following a change of ownership, when North Western Road Car was formed prior to deregulation, it was closed in 1987. A supermarket store now occupies the site although the frontage has been retained. MCCW-bodied Leyland PD3/5s Nos 1745/80/99 and 1839 are seen on 15 August 1976. The bus station stands were on the left.

Ribble's Skelhorne Street combined bus station and garage in Liverpool was opened in July 1960. Built on two levels it catered for both local stage and express coach services which had previously been using on-street bus stands. Leyland PD3/5 No. 1827 is seen departing on 17 July 1978. It was destined to have a short life and was closed by North Western in 1989. The site has subsequently been redeveloped.

A new Ribble garage was opened in The Ellers, in Ulverston, in 1933, to cater for the company's expanding network of services in North Lancashire. Comprising a modest size running/servicing shed and an open parking yard, it could accommodate around thirty vehicles. Leyland Leopards Nos 521, 476, 527 and 493 form the front line of buses crammed into the yard on Saturday 28 May 1977. Following the takeover by Stagecoach the garage was closed in February 1990 and operations were centred on Barrow.

There were two Ribble garages in Blackburn. Foundry Hill garage was acquired with the business of Pendle Motor Services in 1926, while a new garage was opened nearby in George Street East in 1928. The latter was enlarged in 1985 to accommodate the full allocation with Foundry Hill closing at the same time. Ribble was one of Stagecoach's early acquisitions, passing to the Scottish Group on 21 April 1989. Volvo B6 No. 237 is seen on 13 March 1994. Stagecoach sold the Blackburn operations to Transdev in April 2001 and George Street was closed in 2011 with the buses moving to the former Corporation garage at Intack.

Lincolnshire RoadCar was formed in 1928 and established depots throughout the county. The garage in Skegness was located in Grosvenor Road. The company was acquired by the Yorkshire Traction Group in 1988 which later passed to Stagecoach in December 2005. The garage was closed in September 2009 when a new garage was opened in Burgh Road. The building was still in use in 2019 by a scaffolding firm. Bristol MW No. 2242 and FS5G No. 2521, the former still in Lincolnshire green, were parked in the yard on 22 June 1974.

Combined bus stations and garages were not that unusual, and this 1950s structure was located in St Mark Street in Lincoln. Lincolnshire RoadCar Bristol MWs Nos 2083 and 2276 (originally West Yorkshire No. EUG82) were among the buses present on 22 May 1976. The building was demolished in 1995 and the site is now occupied by a new Debenhams store. The RoadCar garage was later relocated in Great Northern Terrace and was still in use by Stagecoach in 2019.

Crosville's Ellesmere Port garage was opened in 1962 and was originally an outstation of Rock Ferry. Buses were parked adjacent to the bus station in Marina Drive. The site was redeveloped in 1972 and the parking area moved to Wellington Road with buses now maintained at Chester. There seems to have been a coming together of these two Bristol VRTs, Nos DVG566/7 (formerly East Midland Nos D101/3), in this 1 April 1984 view. Not long after this picture was taken the buses were parked in a more secure area in Meadow Lane. Following deregulation and the breakup of the Crosville Empire, the Wirral operations were sold to Potteries Motor Traction in February 1990. Facilities were rationalised and Ellesmere Port garage was closed. Operations in the area later passed to FirstBus and then Stagecoach.

The Crosville Empire covered large areas of Wales, Cheshire and parts of Merseyside and the operator had a considerable number of depots and outstations. Wrexham garage in Mold Road was opened in 1933 and closed in 1991 as part of the systematic dismantling of the once mighty Crosville bus company. Former stage vehicles, 1956 Bristol Lodekkas Nos DLG816/06, are seen parked on the garage forecourt on 2 September 1981. Wrexham FC's ground is situated on the opposite side of the road.

The Crosville bus garage in Chester was situated in Liverpool Road and was opened in 1927. The garage survived the systematic breakup of the company and eventually passed into Stagecoach ownership. It was closed as recently as April 2018 with operations being moved to a new depot at Waverton on the outskirts of the city. The site has since been sold for redevelopment.

London Country, with over thirty garages, was absorbed into the National Bus Company on 1 January 1970. Leatherhead garage was opened on 1 June 1925. It was enlarged in 1938 and gained extra open parking space in the mid-1950s. The original buildings were later replaced by a new maintenance shed. Having been acquired by the Drawlane Group in 1988, it was closed on 30 April 1999. The site is now occupied by a new office complex and fire station. On 6 December 1976, on-loan Bournemouth Weymann-bodied Daimler Fleetline No. 199 was rubbing shoulders with LCBS Park Royal-bodied Leyland Atlantean No. AN36.

London County's Staines bus garage, in London Road, was opened in June 1936. It was one of a number of garages designed by Wallis, Gilbert & Partners on the instruction of Frank Pick, the Chief Executive of the recently formed LPTB. Closure came in 1996 and the site is now occupied by an office complex known as Centurion House. On Saturday 4 December 1976 the wintry sun glints off the sides of Regent RTs Nos 3607 and 4496.

Dartford bus garage in Priory Road was opened in 1927 by the Maidstone & District bus company. It was taken over by the LPTB on 1 July 1933. As the road name suggests, it was built on land which had formed part of Dartford Priory which can be traced back to 1346. The garage was closed on 18 January 1986 and the site is now occupied by a DIY superstore. RML2342 entered service from Northfleet garage in November 1965 and remained there until it passed to London Transport in October 1979. It is seen in Priory Road on 13 January 1979.

Eastern Counties (first registered on 30 August 1919) opened a garage in Foundation Street in Ipswich in November 1933. ECW-bodied Bristol MWs Nos L611/44 are seen on the garage forecourt on 19 April 1975. The garage was swept away to make way for the Buttermarket Street Shopping Centre complex which was opened on 1 October 1992. Eastern Counties was sold to the GRT Group in July 1994, ultimately becoming part of FirstBus.

Eastern National had two garage premises in Southend. There was a combined garage/bus station in Queensway and a garage in Fairfax Drive in Prittlewell. The latter dated from the early 1930s and is where 1953 open-top Bristol KSW5G No. 2379 (originally new to Westcliffe-on-Sea Motor Services) could be seen on 9 June 1977. The garage was extended in the 1950s and passed to FirstBus in the mid-1990s. It was later vacated with operations being moved to Hadleigh. After being used for other purposes the building was demolished *c.* 2018.

Aldershot & District merged with Thames Valley to form Alder Valley on 1 January 1972. Still in its original livery Weymann-bodied Dennis Loline No. 818 (A&D No. 508) is seen at the Halimote Road garage in Aldershot on 7 September 1974. The first garage on this site, a somewhat moderately sized structure, was built in 1908. Halimote Road became part of Alder Valley South which was acquired by Stagecoach on 26 October 1992. Although the original buildings have been demolished Stagecoach still had a presence on the site in 2019.

Midland Red opened a new garage in Wellington in July 1932, and it was built on the site of a former nursery with access from Charlton Street. It was rebuilt and modernised in 1953. An extensive line of Plaxton-bodied Fords, headed by No. 382, was parked in the yard on 17 April 1976. The then Midland Red North was acquired by the Drawlane Group in January 1988, later becoming Arriva. The garage was closed in April 2012 and demolished three years later. New residential housing known as Midland Mews now occupies the site.

As the Ribble Empire grew throughout the 1920s and early 1930s, garage premises in Goodwin Street in Bolton were acquired in 1929. This moderately sized garage never had an allocation of more than thirty buses until after deregulation when its importance, due to its location on the edge of the Greater Manchester conurbation, suddenly magnified. The allocation quickly trebled and as can be seen in this 22 April 1990 view, buses spilled out onto the adjoining highway; Renault No. 635 leads the line. The garage later had several owners passing to Transdev, Blue Bus and then Arriva who was the incumbent operator in 2019.

Ribble had opened a garage in Talbot Road in Blackpool in 1933. However, as the coaching side of the business rapidly grew during the 1930s, additional premises were urgently needed, and a much bigger garage was opened in Devonshire Road in 1937. For many years it was the principal home for the Standerwick subsidiary fleet. ECW-bodied Bristol VRLs Nos 70/3 and Plaxton-bodied Leyland Leopard No. 97 are enjoying their winter slumber on 8 January 1977. Following the devolution of the coaching operations the garage was closed in 1987. It was subsequently demolished, and the site has since been redeveloped.

The Brighton Hove & Preston United bus company was formed in 1884. The first motorbuses were operated in 1903 and by 1909 a small garage had been established in Conway Street in Hove. The garage was extended in 1930 and a second garage had been added by 1937. The complex was later further extended. The operator merged with Southdown in January 1969. However, Brighton Hove & District was resurrected in 1985 and was part of the Go-Ahead Group in 2019 with the garage still in use. Southdown Bristol FSF No. 2030 (originally BH&D) and NCME-bodied Daimler CRG No. 2107 are seen in Conway Street on 19 October 1974.

A new garage was opened by Southdown in the Hilsea district of Portsmouth in the 1930s. It survived until 1990 when it was closed following the sale of the company to Portsmouth CityBus. It was subsequently used as a depot for Milk Floats before eventually falling foul of the wreckers' ball in July 2013. The site has been redeveloped with new flats known as Southdown View. A new FirstBus depot was set-up directly opposite. One of Southdown's 'Queen Mary' NCME-bodied Leyland PD3/4s, No. 423, was still sporting the old colours in this 4 June 1975 view.

Former London Transport Daimler Fleetline No. DM1747 (Midland Red No. 2747) is seen back on home territory inside Stamford Brook garage on 3 July 1983. Built on the site of a horse tram depot, which was originally established in 1883, it was home to the London United Tramway cars from 1901. Many years later it was used as a base for the BEA Airport buses. After falling into disuse, it was reopened on 10 May 1980 and was a London United base in 2019.

Yorkshire Traction's Sheffield Road bus garage was originally the Barnsley & District Tramway's electric tramcar depot, which was opened in 1902. YTC was the subject of a management buyout in 1987. Expansion followed with the acquisition of several other bus companies but the YTC Group was eventually taken over by Stagecoach in December 2005. The garage, colloquially known as 'Tracky Sheds', was closed on 22 October 2008. Residential housing, known as Bluebell Bank, now occupies the site. Former Ribble/Standerwick Plaxton-bodied Leyland Leopard No. 876S (YTC No. 38) is seen on 10 September 1979.

The Wakefield & District Light Railway opened an electric tram depot in Barnsley Road in August 1904. The trams ceased to run in July 1932 and the depot was adapted for the West Riding Automobile Company, which was the bus operating arm of the Yorkshire Electric Tramways. The company was first sold to Caldaire Holdings in 1995 which metamorphosed into Arriva. Roe-bodied Guy Arab IV service vehicle No. A14 (previously Nos 458/855) is seen in the yard on 1 June 1975.

Cumberland Motor Services ECW-bodied Bristol FLF No. 525 was recorded parked opposite the Bransty Row garage in Whitehaven on 22 April 1979. The garage was of Art Deco design and was opened in 1931. CMS was taken over by Stagecoach on 22 July 1987. The garage was modernised in 1991 but closed in 2005. It has since remained unused, but plans had been lodged to incorporate the building into a new multimillion-pound redevelopment scheme. The parking area was being used as a car park in 2019.

A line-up of Bristol REs and MWs is seen in the Gadlys garage yard at Aberdare on 2 June 1975. Red & White Services Ltd was formed in June 1929 and Gadlys was one of sixteen depots; the head office was at Chepstow. The operator was merged with Western Welsh in April 1978 to form National Welsh. The company was taken over by Stagecoach on 10 December 1993. The garage was subsequently closed, and operations were moved to nearby Three Oaks.

The former Maidstone & District garage at Silverhill in Hastings was originally built as an electric tram depot for the Hastings & District Tramways and was opened in July 1905. The trams were replaced by trolleybuses in May 1929, which in turn ceased to operate in 1957. Maidstone & District was acquired by British Bus in 1995, passing to the Cowie Group (Arriva) a year later. However, the East Kent operations were acquired by Stagecoach in 2012. The original tram shed still formed part of the depot in 2019. Weymann-bodied Atlantean No. 6443 (DL43) was present on 3 June 1975.

Douglas Corporation acquired the town's horse tramway on 2 January 1902 and purchased its first motorbus in 1914. From 1920 onwards the bus fleet expanded with the first double-deck buses entering the fleet in 1933. A large fleet of AEC Regent IIIs was assembled after the Second World War and some of these were still running when the operator was merged with Isle of Man Road Services on 1 October 1976. The garage was situated close to the town centre in York Road. Some years later it was subsequently closed, and a new residential complex now occupies the site. Duple Midland-bodied Bedford VAS No. 7, new in 1966, is seen at the side of the garage on 14 June 1975.

Isle of Man Road Services was formed in the late 1920s and was originally a motor transport arm of the Isle of Man Railway Company, which was set up to fend off competing bus services with the railway's then near monopoly of island transportation. The Douglas garage was established in Salisbury Street, which was literally just around the corner from the Douglas Corporation garage. On 14 June 1975 former Stratford Blue/Midland Red Willowbrook-bodied Leyland PD3A/1 No. 64 was caught in the garage. Numbers 19 and 55 can be seen on the left.

Following the formation of the Isle of Man National Transport Company on 1 October 1976, both depots were eventually superceded by new facilities adjacent to the steam railway complex. Again, seen on 14 June 1975 MCCW-bodied Leyland PD3A/1 No. 67 and PD2/1 No. 61 were resting in the yard. While this area of the garage now forms a communal drive to a new residential development the main garage building was still standing in 2019.

While the main garage was located in Douglas, buses were also out-stationed at Ramsey, Peel and Port Erin. As can be seen in this view, the Princes Road garage at Ramsey also served as a bus station. On 17 June 1978 Leyland Nationals Nos 14/5, which were new in 1975, were waiting their next turns of duty. In 2019 this view was completely unchanged although the company was then trading as Bus Vannin.

Another view at Ramsey, which dates from 21 August 1982, sees two former Ribble Motors' Marshall-bodied short Leyland Leopards parked in the yard alongside the main garage building. Numbers 1 and 5 in the IOMNT fleet, they were previously Ribble Nos 660/3. Acquired in 1980/79, respectively, they were part of a batch of ten. Apart from the buses the only change to this view in the intervening thirty-seven years is that the yard has received a tarmac surface.

Very reminiscent of Ribble's Garstang garage was the Road Services garage in Atholl Street at Peel, which again also performed the function of a bus station. On 14 June 1975 the occupants were Leyland Royal Tiger No. 90, Weymann-bodied Tiger Cub No. 8 and MCCW-bodied Leyland PD3/1s Nos 31–3, all of which dated from the 1950s. Dating from before the Second World War, Peel garage was closed as an operational base in 2010 but was still standing in 2019.

Lord Street Bus Park, close to Douglas Bus Station, was used by Douglas Corporation to park up out-of-service buses rather than incurring dead mileage with a return trip to the garage. Following the merger of operators in October 1976 the plot continued to be used by the IOMNT. Seen on 28 May 1983 are Leyland National No. 16, PD3A/1 No. 51 and former borough of Preston Panther No. 81 (PBT No. 227). The building behind the buses has since been demolished and the site was in use as a car park in 2019. Lord Street Bus Station was swept away in 2002 and services have since used on-street bus stands.

There had once been an extensive area of sidings alongside Douglas steam railway station. From around 1978/9 this cleared site was used by the recently formed Isle of Man National Transport to park up the majority of the fleet overnight. The area remained in this basic state until 1999 when redevelopment work took place and what is known as the 'Banks Circus' transport headquarters was established, which included a new bus maintenance facility. This enabled the former depots at York Road and Salisbury Street to be closed. Seen in the station yard on 28 May 1983 are IOMNT withdrawn Leyland PD3A/1s Nos 72, 49 and 74.

The St Helens & District Tramway Company opened a horse tram depot in Hall Street in 1881. It was rebuilt to accommodate electric trams in 1899. The Corporation didn't take charge of the system until 1 October 1919. Motorbuses were first operated in 1923 and trolleybuses were introduced in 1927 with all three types sharing the same depot. The garage was extended in 1929 with new maintenance facilities accessed from Torver Street. It closed as a bus garage in 1984 but in 2019 was home to the North West Museum of Transport. St Helens didn't join the MPTE until April 1974 and ELC-bodied Leyland PD2/47 No. 52 was captured just a year later.

The trams had finished in March 1936 with both buses and trolleybuses taking over on the former tram routes. A second garage was established in Jackson Street in 1947. Withdrawn former St Helens buses Nos 27, 14, 48, 13, 49/4 and Birkenhead No. 61 (accident damaged) were to be found at the side of the garage on 18 February 1978. New workshop facilities were added in 1984. Merseyside Transport Ltd had been formed in 1993 and MTL North (created in 1998) was acquired by Arriva on 17 February 2000, with the depot still being in use in 2019.

In the late nineteenth century, a horse-drawn tramway system had evolved in Liverpool operated by the Liverpool Tramways (& Omnibus) Company. A depot had been established in Spellow Lane at Walton as early as 1885. On cessation of the horse trams a new electric tramcar depot was built on the same site. Liverpool's trams weren't phased out until the 1950s and the depot was again rebuilt as a bus garage in 1963. It was closed on 1 July 1989 and the site has since been redeveloped. Originally ordered by Birkenhead, single-deck NCME-bodied Atlantean No. 95 is seen inside on 26 April 1981.

The MPTE bus garage in Linacre Road at Litherland also had a long pedigree and was first opened as a horse-tram depot on 25 November 1882. Later electric trams were accommodated before these were ousted in December 1950. The garage was a victim of bus deregulation and was closed on 26 October 1986. On 19 March 1976 Liverpool's first production Atlantean No. L501 could be seen rubbing shoulders with PD2/20 No. L251 and Bristol RESL No. 2094.

Another electric tram depot was built in Edge Lane. However, this site was chosen for the construction of a new factory where not only were the trams given a heavy overhaul, but completely new trams were also constructed. This expansive facility was opened on 23 October 1928. New bus bodies were assembled in the 1950s and it continued as a bus repair works until closure in 1996. An operational tram depot/bus garage was also attached to the complex. On 30 August 1976 Leyland Atlanteans Nos L516/54/43 were parked in the yard. Latterly in the ownership of MTL Ltd, this cathedral of a building has since been demolished.

As Liverpool's electric tramway continued to expand a tramcar depot was opened in Speke Road at Garston in the early part of the twentieth century. The last trams left the depot on 6 June 1953 and thereafter the building was used solely to garage motorbuses. It was closed in August 1996 and the site has since been redeveloped with blocks of low-rise flats. Alexander-bodied Leyland Atlantean No. 1521 stands out from the crowd on 26 April 1981.

Liverpool Corporation opened a new bus garage in Shaw Road at Speke in 1957. It later passed to Merseyside Transport Limited and then to Arriva in February 2000. The original garage was demolished, and a new depot complex was constructed on the same site in 2012 at a cost of £3.9 million; it was designed to accommodate 150 buses. On 1 April 1984 Alexander-bodied Dennis Dominator No. 0035 is seen inside the original garage building.

Wallasey Corporation commenced operating electric trams from a depot in Seaview Road in 1902. It was sited next to the Corporation's Liscard Pumping Station. The former tramway pits are still discernible in this view of MCCW-bodied Leyland Atlanteans Nos 204/01, which are seen in the original tram shed on 1 May 1976; a separate additional tram/bus shed was built in 1929 on adjacent land. The Merseyside PTE depot was closed following deregulation in 1986 and the site is now occupied by a supermarket.

Bilston and Cleveland Road depots in Wolverhampton were actually sited opposite each other. While the former was opened as a bus garage in 1931, the latter began life as a tram depot in 1902. Former Wolverhampton Corporation MCCW-bodied Guy Arab IV No. 48N has been rescued by the tow truck on 30 March 1976. The pub in the background was the Red Cow, while the bus to the right is in a separate yard which used to be the site of a livestock auction mart. Although the depots were vacated in October 1993 they weren't demolished until 2017.

The former Corporation bus garage in Fox Hollies Road at Acocks Green was opened in June 1928. Its location contributed to the fact that the garage has always provided buses for the Outer Circle routes 11A/C. Seen at the garage entrance on 24 August 1976 is former Birmingham City Transport 1952 MCCW-bodied Guy Arab IV No. 2902. The garage looked no different in 2019 when services were operated by National Express.

Harborne garage was another depot that in its day provided buses for the Outer Circle routes. It was the first purpose-built Corporation bus garage and was opened in 1926. Birmingham Standards Nos 2939/34 and 3022/24 formed this line on 26 February 1977, in the last year of operation of the type by the PTE. Harborne garage did not survive the test of time and was closed in 1986. The site is now occupied by Timber Mill Court Sheltered Accommodation.

Saturday 13 July 1974 sees rows of Daimler Fleetlines lined up in Miller Street garage yard. The buses on show comprise WMPTE Nos 3524/624, 4158 and 3495/517/08/308. Miller Street was opened by Birmingham Corporation as an electric tram depot in January 1904. The trams left in July 1953 and it continued to function as a bus garage until 30 May 2009. Although no longer used as a bus garage the building has been divided into smaller industrial units.

Above and below: Coventry Corporation Tramways commenced operating electric trams on 1 January 1912 after taking over from the Electric Tramways Company. Depots were located at Priestly Bridge and Foleshill. In 1921 a purpose-built bus garage was opened in Harnal Lane East. Such was the extent of this garage that the land at the back actually connected through to Priestly Bridge tram depot. On the night of 14 November 1940, the city of Coventry suffered a devastating air raid attack from which the tramway never recovered. Buses were borrowed to replace the trams and operations were concentrated at Foleshill and Harnal Lane until Sandy Lane garage was opened in 1954, with the former closing at the same time. On 13 February 1983 MCW Metrobuses, Nos 2462/612/4/466/106, take refuge inside the garage, while former Coventry Fleetlines Nos 1039/31/75 are not so lucky and are exposed to the snowy elements in the yard. The site of Priestly Bridge tram depot is now occupied by a mosque, while both Harnal Lane and Sandy Lane were closed in 1986 following the opening of a new garage at Pool Meadow, which was still in use by National Express in 2019.

Metrobus (West Yorkshire PTE) NCME-bodied Daimler CRG No. 3090 heads a line of buses at Skircoat Road bus garage in Halifax on 20 March 1983. The depot was built as an electric tram shed and opened in June 1898. It was converted into a bus garage following cessation of the trams in February 1939. A separate garage, known as Elmwood, was later built on the opposite side of Huddersfield Road. Both garages were still in use by FirstBus in 2019.

Huddersfield Corporation commenced operation of electric trams on 14 February 1901 from a depot at Longroyd Bridge. A second depot was later opened at Great Northern Street. Longroyd Bridge was increased in size in July 1921 with the opening of an additional building which was built on the site of Victoria Gardens. A new garage was later constructed on the combined site but was closed in 1986. Former Huddersfield Corporation Roe-bodied Daimler CVG6 No. 4444 is seen inside the St Thomas' Road garage (Longroyd Bridge) on 18 January 1975.

Above and below: Bradford Corporation commenced running electric trams on 30 June 1898 and established six depots. While the trams didn't finish until 1950, trolleybuses were introduced as early as 1911 and the system was the last to operate in the UK, closing on 26 March 1972. A sizeable fleet of motorbuses was also operated, and a purpose-built garage was constructed *c.* 1930 on land which had previously been occupied by the Corporation's gas works. The access was in Ludlam Street. An open parking yard was later established on adjacent land which swallowed up what had previously been Castle Street, Moss Street and Lower Thomas Street. Two views taken on 10 December 1977 depict former Bradford Daimler CRGs Nos 2406/27 (above) and Regent Vs Nos 2186/4 (below). A new garage was opened in the city centre in 1977, known as Hall Ings. Ludlam Street enjoyed a brief spell as home to the West Yorkshire Transport Museum which was opened in 1984. However, it was later vacated but the depot was occupied by industrial units in 2019.

Sovereign Street garage in the centre of Leeds was opened as an electric tram depot *c.* 1910. It was later enlarged and much later still converted into a bus garage following abandonment of the tramway during the 1950s. Absorbed into the West Yorkshire PTE in April 1974 the garage was closed after deregulation and demolished in 1989. Still wearing Leeds City Transport two-tone green Roe-bodied Atlanteans, Nos 498 and 521 were parked in the yard on 23 February 1975.

Middleton garage was a much more recent addition and was constructed during the 1950s to garage the tramway replacement buses. It had a capacity for over 150 buses. On Sunday 20 March 1983 Atlanteans Nos 581/72/19, 427, 501, 418, 582, 417, 554, 6334 and 571/20 were lined up ready for the Monday morning services. The garage was closed on 25 October 1986 and although subsequently demolished the site had not been redeveloped by 2019.

As the tramway system was gradually abandoned during the 1950s, the depots at Chapeltown, Kirkstall Road and Stanley Road were all closed. Another new garage, a somewhat low-budget affair, was opened on the then fledgling Seacroft Industrial Estate, in 1956. Parked under the lean-to on 23 February 1975 was a collection of back-loaders consisting of a mixture of AECs, Daimlers and Titans Nos 882/4, 113, 706, 282, 702, 111, 891/3, 919, 887 and 970. The garage was closed in 1983 but has since found use as a highways depot for Leeds City Council.

Otley Road garage at Headingley could trace its roots back to 1873 when a horse tram depot was opened on the site by the Leeds Tramway Company. In the early years of the twentieth century it was rebuilt as an electric tram depot and subsequently rebuilt and enlarged in 1935. It was converted to a bus garage *c.* 1956, and further enlarged during the 1970s, but was later closed and the site had been redeveloped with a complex of retirement homes by 1993. A retiring row of former LCT AEC Regent Vs stands in the winter gloom on 23 February 1975.

Torre Road tram depot in Leeds was opened as late as May 1937. The original running shed was constructed of concrete segments. From April 1955 it catered for buses only and an additional garage building and open parking yard was added. MCW Metrobus No. 7527 can be seen on 20 March 1983, with the distinctive windows behind which still identified the building from the outside in 2019, although it is no longer a bus garage and is in use as a fleet depot for Leeds City Council vehicles.

The original Bramley tram depot was located at the junction of Stanningley Road and Henconner Lane. However, as part of the tramway replacement programme a new bus garage was opened in 1949, on nearby vacant land, which was also accessed from Henconner Lane. In the mid-1970s the yard was being used as a dump by the West Yorkshire PTE for redundant Corporation buses, with former Halifax PD3s Nos 3204/47, Bradford Regent V No. 2135 and Leeds Daimler CVG No. 881 present on 23 February 1975. The garage was still in use by FirstBus in 2019.

Hyde Road tram depot in Manchester was opened in November 1902 and had a capacity for 265 tramcars. A separate building for the repair and construction of trams was built fronting Hyde Road. The last trams departed on 10 January 1949, but it was also used to garage trolleybuses. Following the formation of the PTE the adjacent yard was used by the driver training school. Leyland PD2s, former Ashton No. 5432, Manchester No. 3657 and Leigh No. 6955, were parked up on 1 August 1976. At the time of writing part of the main depot was still in use by Stagecoach in Manchester while most of the other buildings were still standing and occupied.

Following the opening of the initial three tram depots at Queens Road, Hyde Road and Princess Road there was a seventeen-year lull before Parrs Wood bus garage was opened in 1926 followed by Birchfields Road two years later. The latter was designed to accommodate both buses and trams. This line-up was present on 9 November 1980 and included Atlanteans Nos 7062/606/827/147, 1150 and former Manchester Daimler CRG No. 4610. Birchfields Road was closed on 25 October 1986; it was subsequently demolished, and the site has been redeveloped.

Oldham Corporation had used a number of depots in the early part of the twentieth century. As the trams were in decline a new bus garage was opened in Wallshaw Street in May 1938 with a capacity for 300 buses. This latterly replaced the depots at Henshaw Street and Hollinwood, while Wallshaw Place tram depot remained open until August 1946, thereafter assuming the role as a bus works. Former North Western AEC Reliance No. 940 heads a line of single-deck types on 3 August 1975. While the works have gone the depot was still in use by FirstBus.

The SHMD Tramways & Electricity Board opened a new electric tram depot in Stalybridge Park Road in 1903. Trams ceased to operate in May 1945 and from 1962 buses were parked on a newly concreted area, which had previously been the reservoir for the electricity generating works and was adjacent to the old tram shed. Former Salford CT MCCW-bodied Leyland PD2/40 No. 3021 is seen on 13 February 1976. A new GM Buses depot was opened in Stalybridge in February 1978. This garage in turn was closed by FirstBus in April 2017.

Northenden garage, in Harling Road at Wythenshawe, was ready for use in 1942. However, the building was requisitioned by the Ministry of Aircraft Production and didn't assume its role as a bus garage until 1946. It was closed on 25 October 1986 but has Grade II listed status and was being used as a covered car park in 2019. Former Manchester Corporation MCCW-bodied Leyland PD2/40 No. 3549 is seen leaving for an evening peak working on 4 May 1976.

Bolton Corporation was initially an operator of electric trams and in the early years boasted six tram depots. In October 1929 a purpose-built bus garage was opened in Crook Street and was built on land formerly occupied by a railway coal yard. Former Corporation buses, Bury Nos 6374/56, Bolton Nos 6622/41 and Rochdale No. 6151 are seen in the graveyard on 18 September 1974. A new garage was opened on the same site in 1979 but this too was closed by the then incumbent operator FirstBus, in March 2004. The houses above are in Fletcher Road and while the garage is no more the nineteenth century dwellings are now looking down on a retail park.

Queens Road was the first electric tram depot opened by Manchester Corporation, on 6 June 1901. Additional small bus garages were added to the rear of the building in 1928 and 1935, while the original tram shed was converted for use as a bus garage in 1938. Following privatisation, the garage was acquired by FirstBus in March 1996, passing to Go-Ahead in 2019. Wrightbus-bodied Volvo B9TLs Nos 37380 and 37442 and B5LH No. 39215 were photographed on 20 March 2016.

Over the years Glasgow Corporation utilised more than thirty depots and garages for their fleets of trams, trolleybuses and motorbuses. One such bus garage was Ibrox Parking Ground which was located in Helen Street, close to Ibrox Park Football Stadium, and was opened in May 1943. The Greater Glasgow PTE was formed on 1 June 1973 and Atlantean No. LA179 is seen in the yard on 10 May 1975. GGPTE later became the Strathclyde PTE and then Strathclyde Buses. The latter was acquired by FirstBus in May 1996. The site is now occupied by a new Police Scotland Operations Complex.

Meanwhile Knightswood bus garage was situated north of the Clyde in Munro Place, just off the Great Western Road, and was opened on 23 October 1932. It had a capacity for 260 buses. Leyland PD2/25 No. L46 was new in 1956 and is seen alongside a somewhat austere looking structure on 10 May 1975. Having been acquired by FirstBus in 1996 the garage was closed in 2004 when a new depot was opened at Scotstoun. It was demolished in 2010 and the extensive site is now occupied by residential housing; the former admin block is a listed building and is still standing.

Doncaster Corporation operated electric trams from June 1902 and had two depots, almost opposite each other, in Grey Friars' Road. The trams finished in 1935. Buses were first operated in 1922 – trolleybuses from 1928 – with the latter replacing the trams. A new garage was opened in Leicester Avenue (née Town Moor Avenue) opposite the racecourse, in 1938. Doncaster Corporation was absorbed by the South Yorkshire PTE on 1 April 1974 and former Corporation 1963-built Leyland Tiger Cub No. 33 (SYPTE No. 1033) is seen alongside the garage on 27 February 1976. Firstbus took control of the privatised company (Mainline Group) in 1995 and a new depot was constructed adjacent to the original buildings with an entrance from Leger Way (née Lonsdale Avenue). The original site is now occupied by a DIY superstore.

Sheffield Corporation Electric Tramways operated out of seven depots. However, when the decision was made to abandon the tramway in 1951 a policy to construct completely new bus garages was implemented. These were established at East Bank, Greenlands, Halfway and Herries Road while Leadmill was the only former tram depot which was converted for use by motorbuses. East Bank was opened on 2 May 1959 at a cost of £450,000 and is where this line of AEC Regent Vs was captured on 31 March 1975. The garage was still in use by FirstBus in 2019.

The Rawtenstall to Bacup Tramway opened a steam tram depot in the town in Bacup Road in 1889. This was acquired by the Corporation and the system electrified in 1909. A second tram depot was built opposite and was opened in 1921. Both depots were also used to garage buses. The original depot was closed in April 1932, while the second depot was enlarged and rebuilt as a bus garage and reopened as such on 1 May 1933. Rawtenstall and Haslingden Corporations were merged on 1 April 1968 to form the Rossendale JTC. The garage remained in use until September 2008 when the operator moved to a new garage in Knowsley Road. 'Rosso' was acquired by Transdev in January 2018. ELC-bodied Leyland Leopard No. 50 was packed tightly in the garage on 9 March 1975. The Bacup Road garage was later demolished.

Eastbourne Corporation commenced operating buses in 1903 and established a small garage in what was then known as Destructor Road. A larger separate garage was built opposite, several years later, in what had now become known as Corporation Road. This was enlarged in the late 1920s by which time the road had been renamed for a second time and was now known as Churchdale Road. The building had an imposing brick frontage. The garage remained here for many years until a new depot was constructed in Birch Road and the original site was redeveloped. Eastbourne Buses was acquired by Stagecoach on 18 December 2008. Five of Eastbourne's 1962/3 ELC-bodied AEC Regent Vs were neatly lined up on 8 June 1977.

Llandudno UDC commenced operating Tourist Services in July 1928 but never operated any stagecarriage services. The small fleet of diminutive buses was housed in a garage in Builder Street West. On 1 April 1974 the authority was renamed Aberconwy UDC. AJC 550 was one of a trio of twenty-four-seat Metalcraft-bodied Guy Wolfs purchased in 1951. It is seen in the garage yard on 19 June 1976. The UDC ceased operating buses in 1999 and the garage has since been demolished with the site now occupied by a maintenance contractor's depot.

A depot complex was first established at Rigby Road in Blackpool in 1920 but initially it consisted of works facilities for the maintenance of the trams. The tram depot opposite was known as Blundell Street and had been opened in 1885. A tram traverser and works buildings had previously occupied what later became an open parking yard for the buses, although the buildings facing the above line of MCCW-bodied Leyland PD3A/1s were still in use for buses and trams in 2019. Seen on 13 March 1977 are Titans Nos 527/3/1/18/40 and 354/80/77/6/57.

A separate bus garage was added to the complex in 1925 with a capacity for over 100 buses. A new tramcar building was constructed adjacent to the bus garage and opened in 1935. This was followed by a new office block in the north-west corner of the site a couple of years later. Some of the original buildings, as seen beyond the buses in the top picture, were demolished in the 1980s to create additional car parking space. Finally, a new bus maintenance building was constructed on the east side of the yard in 1985. Blackpool Transport Services was the last remaining local authority-owned bus operator in Lancashire in 2019. DAF No. 351 and Dennis Trident No. 358 portray the old livery on 24 August 2017.

Swindon Corporation Tramways commenced operation of electric trams from a newly constructed depot in Corporation Street on 22 September 1904. Following the cessation of the tramway in July 1929 a new bus garage was built on an enlarged plot which incorporated an open parking lot. The depot was rebuilt in the mid-1980s. However, operations were moved to a new depot in Barnfield Road in July 2005 and Thamesdown Transport was acquired by Go-Ahead in 2017. Leyland PD2A/24 No. 128 is seen in the garage yard on 18 October 1977.

Cardiff Corporation first opened an electric tram depot in Newport Road at Roath in May 1902. Trolleybuses were purchased to operate the last tram routes, and these were garaged at Roath and a depot in Clare Road. A purpose-built bus garage was opened in Sloper Road *c.* 1932 with a capacity for 180 buses. This was later extended, and an open parking yard was added. In 2019 it was home to all 240 buses of the Cardiff Bus fleet. AEC Regent V No. 410 and Guy Arab Vs Nos 452/27 are seen parked in the yard on 2 July 1977.

Shirley electric tram depot in Southampton was built on the site of a former horse tram depot and opened in January 1900. Following the demise of the trams in December 1949 it was converted into a bus garage and reopened as such on 16 July 1950. Southampton City Transport Leyland PD2/27 No. 305 and AEC Regent V No. 402 were at the front of the garage on 22 July 1974. Closure came on 28 March 1982. Residential housing now occupies the site.

Portswood electric tram depot was also built on the site of a former horse tram depot which was first established in May 1879. Between 1908 and 1930 the Corporation built all its own trams at this site. Two separate bus garages were added in 1928 and 1931. The extensive site was redeveloped and reconfigured between 1973 and 1981, enabling the whole fleet of over 200 buses to be garaged there. The garage latterly passed to FirstBus and was closed after service on 28 August 2010. The site is now occupied by a supermarket store. Two months old ELC-bodied Leyland AN68A/1R No. 205 was taking a rest from service on 3 June 1977.

Abbey Meadow in Abbey Park Road was the chosen site for Leicester Corporation's electric tram depot which opened in May 1904. Rebuilding work was undertaken in 1926 to accommodate the Corporation's growing fleet of motorbuses. Rebranded as Leicester City Bus in 1983 the operator was sold to the GRT Group in November 1993, which became FirstBus in April 1995. This characteristic garage was closed on 12 May 2007 and demolished three years later. Former Leeds City Transport Daimler CVG6LX/30 7517 UA was being used by Hestair Dennis as a testbed and was present in the garage on 3 March 1976.

LCT also had an office block with an adjacent parking ground in Rutland Street in the city centre. Opened in 1969 the complex was closed around 1987. The office building was demolished in 2002 to make way for the Leicester Cultural Business Centre. The crew of 1967 Leyland PD3A/12 No. 16 proudly pose for pictures on the occasion of the last rear-entrance buses bowing out of service on 2 October 1982.

The Blackpool, St Annes & Lytham Tramways Company had two depots; one in Squires Gate Lane and one in Henry Street in Lytham (closed in 1903). The original shed in SGL was on the north side and was replaced by a new depot on the south side in June 1904. Lytham St Annes Corporation was formed on 9 November 1922, later becoming Fylde Borough Transport and then Blue Buses. Blue Buses was acquired by Blackpool TS on 22 December 1993 and was run as a subsidiary until 1996. The garage was closed in April 1999 and the site has since been redeveloped. NCME-bodied Leyland PD2/20 No. 57 is seen on 26 March 1975.

Burnley & District Tramways opened a horse tram depot at Queensgate on 17 September 1881. Following acquisition by the Corporation, an electric tram depot was constructed on the same site and opened in January 1902. The BCN JTC was formed on 1 April 1933 and became Burnley & Pendle forty-one years later. Stagecoach finally completed the full purchase of the operator on 8 March 1997, but the company was then sold on to Blazefield Holdings (Transdev) in April 2001. Former Sunderland Bristol RELL, Burnley & Pendle No. 83, is seen on 16 July 1980.

Darlington Corporation opened a new electric tram depot in Haughton Road in June 1904. It was built in the shadow of the town's newly constructed power station (1900–76). The trams were replaced by trolleybuses in 1926. While the original tram shed was converted for use by trolleybuses/motorbuses, an extension was built between the tram shed and Haughton Road, *c*. 1930. Roe-bodied Daimler CCG5s Nos 7 and 9 were over the pits on 19 April 1980. After a bitter competitive battle for passengers, the operator went into liquidation on 9 November 1994. The garage was subsequently demolished, and a fitness centre has been built in its place.

Warrington Corporation opened an electric tram depot in Mersey Street in April 1902. A purpose-built bus garage was built adjacent in 1930. In 1947 additional premises were acquired in Wilderspool Causeway. The offices and maintenance facilities were added in the early 1960s and the Mersey Street premises were vacated. ELC-bodied Leyland PD2/40 No. 41 is seen at the front of the garage on 18 February 1978. The garage was still in use by the operator in 2019 although proposals had been put forward to move to a new site.

Above and below: Milehouse in Plymouth was originally the site of the Plymouth Stonehouse and Davenport Tramways electric tram depot, which was opened in November 1901. This replaced a former horse tram depot which had been located at Millbay. The original Plymouth Corporation tram depots were situated at Compton Road and Prince Rock. The PS&D Company was taken over by Plymouth Corporation on 1 July 1922 and the Milehouse site was acquired. The trams ceased to operate on 29 September 1945 and a bus garage was established on the site which included an extensive open parking area. In the picture above, Plymouth Citybus Atlanteans Nos 77, 152, 80/5 are seen at rest on 7 August 1985, while twenty-five years later the emphasis was on single-decker types with a row of Plaxton-bodied Volvo B6s, including Nos 53, 30, 20/2, 17 and 32, neatly lined up on 6 March 2010. In 2019 the operator was part of the Go-Ahead Group.

Lancaster Corporation commenced operating electric trams from a depot in Thurnham Street on 14 January 1903. As the fleet of motorbuses increased and eventually ousted the trams, operations were moved to a new depot in Kingsway which opened in July 1937. The garage was closed on 21 August 1993 following the takeover of City of Lancaster Transport by Stagecoach. It remained in the ownership of the council and, as a Grade II listed building, it has been incorporated into a new development. Veteran Daimler CVG5 No. 466 is seen on 27 May 1975.

An eclectic mix of backends is featured in this picture taken inside the former Morecambe & Heysham Corporation bus garage on 18 July 1978. Opened on 19 May 1939 it was built on the site of two former adjacent tramway depots. Ownership passed to Stagecoach on 22 August 1993 and the garage was closed in 1996 when a new depot was opened on the White Lund Trading Estate. The garage site has since been redeveloped.

Portsmouth Corporation's North End tram depot was built on the site of the former Portsmouth Street Tramways Company's horse tram depot, which can be traced back to the mid-1870s. It was opened in September 1901 and later converted for use as a bus garage. It was closed on 31 October 1981 with all operations being moved to Eastney. The site has since been redeveloped with residential housing. Leyland Panther Cubs Nos 150/61 were present on 4 June 1975.

Extensions to the tramway system were made in 1909 and 1913 and a second tram depot was opened in the district of Eastney. It too was converted into a bus garage after the trams ceased to operate. MCCW-bodied Leyland Atlantean No. 225 and Marshall-bodied AEC Swift No. 178 were captured in the yard on 12 June 1976. Following a brief period under Stagecoach ownership the company passed to Transit Holdings in 1991. However, Eastney garage was closed soon afterwards, on 25 May, and the site has since been redeveloped.

Caerphilly Urban District Council was granted powers to run buses in May 1917. A garage was built on the site of a former Laundry in the shadow of the gas works in Mill Road. On 1 April 1974 the UDC operators of Caerphilly, Bedwas & Machen and Gelligaer were combined to form Rhymney Valley District Council Transport with a new livery of brown, gold and cream, as seen on Leyland Leopard No. 97 (ex-B&M No. 7). Leyland PD2/37 No. 35. RVDC was acquired by National Welsh in March 1989. The Caerphilly garage and the gas works have long since been replaced by residential housing.

Taff Ely Transport (formerly Pontypridd UDC) Roe-bodied AEC Reliances Nos 85/4 are flanked by Scania No. 15 and AEC Regent No. 4 in this 14 April 1976 view of the garage yard. Pontypridd commenced running electric trams on 6 March 1905. These were superceded by first trolleybuses and then motorbuses. The operator was acquired by National Welsh in August 1988, but the garage was closed four years later when NW were placed into administration. The Glyntaff site is now part of the University of South Wales' college campus and the building behind the buses has been sympathetically incorporated into a new development.

Newport Corporation commenced running electric trams on 9 April 1903 from a depot in Corporation Road. While the original shed was set back from the road, an additional bus garage was later added, fronting Corporation Road. The original building was still in use by Newport Bus in 2019 when the size of the bus fleet stood at around 100 vehicles, including the first electric buses to be operated in Wales. In earlier years Newport had favoured Scania buses and MCW Metropolitan No. 117 is seen with Leyland Tiger No. 1 on 15 June 1985.

Another group of Newport buses, but not in Newport as might have been expected. These four Longwell Green-bodied Leyland PD2/40s were photographed in the yard of City of Lancaster's Morecambe garage on 10 August 1974, while the buses were on loan to the operator. A modern complex of low-rise flats known as Mears Beck Close has since been built on this former tram/bus depot site.

Northampton's St James' Road tram depot was opened in July 1904. The trams operated until December 1934 and thereafter the building was used solely as a bus garage. The operator was acquired by the GRT Group in 1993, thereafter becoming part of the FirstBus Group. The garage was closed on 22 October 2013 and was still standing in 2019. Inside, on 31 May 1977, were Roe-bodied Daimler CVG6 No. 244 and preserved NCB-bodied No. 154.

By coincidence, Colchester Corporation Tramways also commenced running electric trams in July 1904 from their depot in Magdalen Road. It was converted into a bus garage in 1928/9. The operator was sold to the Cowie Group in August 1996 and the garage remained in use by Arriva until March 2008. It was later reopened and used by First Essex before being closed for a second time. The building was demolished in December 2018. Colchester Borough Transport AEC Reliance No. 6 (ex-Salford CT No. 106) is seen inside on 19 April 1975.

Nottingham Corporation had four tram depots, the oldest of which was located at Trent Bridge. Opened in 1901 it was also later used for trolleybuses. A second shed was built on the opposite side of Turney Street in 1920, specifically for buses. NCME-bodied Leyland PDR1A No. 528 is seen adjacent to the bus garage on 29 May 1979. While the building behind the bus has been demolished the depot was still in use by Nottingham City Transport in 2019.

(Lower) Parliament Street, also known as Carter Gate, didn't open until 1928 and enjoyed a brief period of tramcar operation until 1936, as evidenced by the tracks which were still insitu when Weymann-bodied AEC Renown No. 363 was photographed alongside the garage on 13 November 1975. This garage also played host to trolleybuses between 1928 and 1966 and like Trent Bridge was still in use by NCT in 2019.

The Blackburn & Over Darwen Tramways Company established a steam tram depot at Intack in the early 1880s. Following acquisition of the company by Blackburn Corporation on 24 August 1898, the depot was converted for use by electric trams from July 1901. The Corporation also acquired a former horse tram depot in Simmons' Street, which also subsequently enjoyed a brief spell of electric tram operation. Nearly a hundred years after the first depot was opened on the site, ELC-bodied Leyland PD2A/24s Nos 41, 39/1 are seen in the bus garage on 19 September 1980.

Blackburn Corporation didn't finally close its tramway system until 3 September 1949. Some twenty-six years later tram tracks were still insitu leading from Accrington Road into the former tram shed. The Transport Department's Guy Arab Recovery Vehicle was caught manoeuvring ELC-bodied Leyland PDR1A/1 No. 53 on 25 August 1975. Although the original garage buildings have been razed to the ground the site was still in use by Transdev in 2019.

The Preston Tramways Company operated horse-drawn trams between 1879 and 1903 from a depot in Fishergate Hill (old Vicarage from 1899). Preston Corporation terminated the lease and opened a new electric tramcar depot, with an adjoining generating station, in Deepdale Road in June 1904. This was extended in 1915. The trams finished in December 1935 and the original shed was converted into a bus garage in 1934/5. Meanwhile an adjacent bus garage was opened in 1932. The complex was extended in 1964 with the addition of further covered accommodation. Seen inside the original tram shed (converted to a dock shop in 1965), on 16 April 2016, are Mercedes Citaro No. 33007, Optare Solo No. 20832 and Wrightbus Streetlite No. 32303. Preston Bus has been part of the Rotala Group since February 2011, following a brief period of ownership by Stagecoach.

Green Triangle Buses (t/a South Lancs Transport) began operations from depot premises in Arley Way on an Industrial Estate in Atherton in 2000. The company was acquired by Rotala on 1 March 2015 and renamed Diamond Bus North West. The depot was run in conjunction with the Preston depot and former Preston Bus Scania ELC-Esteem's Nos 30912/21/11/17–9, seen on 19 March 2017, formed part of the allocation. Rotala later acquired Goodwins of Eccles (stage services) and the FirstBus' Bolton operations. Consequently, from September 2019, Atherton ceased to be used as an operational depot.

Widnes Corporation Transport only ever operated motorbuses and the garage on the corner of Moor Lane and Caldwell Road was opened in 1909. As the garage outgrew the size of the fleet, additional parking was established in an open yard a couple of hundred yards further along Caldwell Road. On 1 April 1974 the name was changed to Halton Transport with the new borough, henceforth administered from Cheshire, now including the town of Runcorn. ELC-bodied Dennis Super Darts Nos 38 and 43 are seen alongside the garage in Caldwell Road on 5 June 2015. Halton Transport ceased trading in January 2020.

Accrington Corporation's garage in Ellison Street was originally the site of the Steam Tramways Company depot which was opened in April 1886. Electric trams were operated between 1908 and 1932. An open parking yard was later established adjacent to the garage, while the operator was renamed Hyndburn Borough Transport in 1974. Following acquisition by Stagecoach on 11 September 1996 the garage was closed sixteen days later; the building, however, has since found other uses. ELC-bodied Leyland PD3A/1 No. 160 is seen over the pits on 3 August 1974.

Barrow Corporation first opened an electric tram depot in Salthouse Road in February 1904. The trams ceased to operate in April 1932 and a new bus garage was built in Hindpool Road, which opened on 10 January 1936. The operator was acquired by Stagecoach on 26 May 1989. Hindpool garage was later closed and demolished and a new depot opened on Walney Road. Massey-bodied Leyland PD2A/27 No. 107 is seen at the front of the garage on 20 April 1976.

Chester City Transport's garage occupied the site of the former Chester Tramway Company's depot, which opened in June 1879. Electric trams were operated from 1903 to 1930 (track still in situ adjacent to the buses). Rebranded ChesterBus in April 2005, the operator was acquired by FirstBus in June 2007. Operations then passed to Stagecoach in January 2013. A new student accommodation block known as 'Tramways' has since been built on the site. Leyland Olympians Nos 11 (ex-A1 Service) and 8 (ex-WYPTE) are seen on 5 July 1992.

Cleveland Transit (first formed on 1 April 1968 as Teesside Municipal Transport) came into being on 1 April 1974 and utilised the former depots of Middlesbrough and Stockton Corporations, and the Rail-less Traction Board's former South Bank trolleybus/motorbus depot. The latter was opened in 1919 and the trolleybuses continued to run until 18 April 1971. Former Teesside RTB Roe-bodied Leyland PD2A/27 No. H236 (TRTB No. 36) is seen at South Bank on 20 May 1978. South Bank was closed in 1986 while Cleveland Transit was acquired by Stagecoach in September 1994, and only the Stockton garage still functions as a bus depot.

Southend Corporation's electric tram depot in London Road, opened in 1901, and was actually located behind other properties and was accessed by a single track which ran along a narrow alley. It was extended in 1931 but the trams ceased to run in April 1942. A new bus garage was opened in 1960 fronting directly onto London Road. Maintenance facilities also existed in Tunbridge Road (1959–93). The operator was acquired by the British Bus Group in July 1993 thereafter passing to the Cowie Group. The garage was closed by Arriva on 28 January 2000 with operations moving to a new depot in Short Street. Southend Transport 1963 Alexander-bodied Albion Lowlander LR7 No. 323 is seen in the expansive bus garage on 3 April 1976.

The Great Grimsby Street Tramways Company commenced operation of an electric tram system on 1 January 1902. The depot was situated in Cleethorpes in Pelham Road. In 1925 Grimsby Corporation purchased that part of the system within their borough and opened a new depot in Victoria Street. The trams finished running on 17 July 1937, but it wasn't until 1957 that the two transport systems were merged with operations then being concentrated at Victoria Street. The company was acquired by Stagecoach in 1993 and the garage was still in use in 2019. Daimlers Nos 104 and 18 (ex-London Transport) are seen on 13 May 1984.

Derby Corporation first operated electric trams from depots in Nottingham Road and Osmaston Road. Both were later used to garage trolleybuses from January 1932 onwards. A new motorbus/trolleybus garage was opened in Ascot Drive in 1949. Osmaston Road and Nottingham Road were later closed, the latter in 1952. Following the acquisition of Blue Bus Service in December 1973, the operating name was changed accordingly in 1986, later changing again to City Rider in 1994. The company was subsequently acquired by Arriva in August 1996 and the garage was still in use in 2019. A number of Daimler CVGs can be seen inside the cavernous building on 24 September 1977.

Lincoln Corporation's first depot was built for the electric trams and was located on the corner of Newark Road and Ellison Street. After the trams finished in March 1929 a new bus garage was opened in November of that year in St Mark Street. As the bus fleet increased in size additional railway land – opposite the garage and accessed from Rope Walk – was used to park up buses. Roe-bodied Atlantean No. 7 is seen among a variety of buses on 30 April 1977. The operator was first sold in 1991 to a consortium then passing to Yorkshire Traction and finally Stagecoach. The garage was demolished in 2002 and the site redeveloped.

Hull originally had five tram depots and, between 1937 and 1964, operated an extensive trolleybus system while the tramway was abandoned in June 1945. While the former tram depots were retained for the buses and trolleybuses, a new central garage was opened in Lombard Street in 1936. On the night of 7 May 1941, the garage suffered a direct hit in an air raid and was not rebuilt until 1952. Hull City Transport was sold to Cleveland Transit in December 1993, becoming part of the Stagecoach Group a year later. Stagecoach established a new garage in a former builders merchants' depot in Foster Street in 1996 and all trace of Central garage has since been erased. AEC Reliance No. 161 is seen on 12 July 1975.

Brighton Corporation Tramways commenced operation of electric trams on 25 November 1901. The tram shed was located in Lewes Road. When the trams finally stopped running in 1939 it was converted into a bus/trolleybus garage. The company was sold to Go-Ahead in May 1997 and the then Brighton Transport was merged with Brighton Hove & District and the latter was still operating from the garage in 2019. Leyland Panther No. 41 is seen on 3 June 1975.

Reading Corporation's Mill Lane tram depot was opened in July 1903. From July 1936 it also played host to trolleybuses while the trams bowed out three years later. The depot originally had its own generating station at the side of the running shed. Reading Transport Ltd moved to a new depot in Great Knollys Street on 19 April 1998 and Mill Lane was demolished almost immediately to make way for the Oracle Shopping Mall. On 5 June 1976 Dennis Loline No. 144 and AEC Regent IIIs Nos 100/92 were to be found in the small adjacent yard. In 2018 the company also served Bracknell, Newbury, Slough and Windsor with a fleet of 192 buses.

Hartlepool Electric Tramways commenced operation from a depot in Cleveland Road in May 1896. The part of the system within its boundaries passed to West Hartlepool Corporation in August 1912, while the remainder was bought by Hartlepool Corporation in 1925. Later trolleybuses were operated, some of which were jointly owned. The two boroughs were eventually merged on 1 April 1967 becoming Hartlepool CBT. Buses were generally parked on open land in the town centre, which is where Leyland PD2 No. 14, Leopard No. 33 and Bristol RE No. 81 could be seen on 7 January 1978. Cleveland Road was replaced by a new garage (Lynn Street) on this site in the early 1980s, but this was vacated after the takeover by Stagecoach.

Chesterfield Corporation's electric tram depot was located in Chatsworth Road and opened in December 1904. The trams finished in May 1927. In 1964 the Corporation moved to a new modern bus garage at Stonegravels which was accessed from Sheffield Road. The operator was taken over by Stagecoach on 27 July 1995 and the garage was still in use in 2019. Former Liverpool Corporation MCCW-bodied Leyland Panther No. 1056 – Chesterfield No. 63 – was among the tightly packed buses on 26 November 1981.

Burton-upon-Trent Corporation Tramways commenced operating electric trams from a depot in Horninglow Street on 13 June 1906. This remained home to the Corporation and subsequent East Staffordshire DC fleets until the operator's merger with Stevensons of Uttoxeter on 1 October 1985. The garage has since been demolished and a police station now occupies the site. Former Bournemouth Tiger Cub No. 267 – ESDC No. 4 – was tucked inside on 24 May 1975.

Ipswich Corporation opened a new electric tram depot in Constantine Road in November 1903, and this has remained the principal home of Ipswich Buses ever since. The original buildings are still in use although land at the rear, which once housed a rubbish destructor, has been incorporated as an open parking yard. AEC Regent Vs Nos 29 and 45 are seen on 19 April 1975. A second depot for trolleybuses was opened at Priory Heath; it is now a transport museum.

Great Yarmouth Corporation Tramways ran in two separate sections divided by the River Yare. Each section had its own depot. The western section closed on 25 September 1930 along with the depot at Gorleston. The trams on the eastern section finished in December 1933 but the depot in Caister Road, opened in June 1902, was subsequently used as a bus garage. In 2019 the garage was still in use by First Eastern Counties. Single-deck Marshall-bodied Leyland Atlantean No. 39 was one of three of the type owned and is seen on 5 June 1975.

Lowestoft Corporation Tramways commenced operation on 22 July 1903 from a four-road depot in Rotterdam Road. The fifteen trams were replaced by motorbuses from 1927–31. On 1 April 1974 Lowestoft Corporation was renamed Waveney District Council with nineteen buses transferring to the new authority. However, the operator was taken over by Eastern Counties on 5 December 1977. Number 5 was a Pennine-bodied AEC Reliance which was acquired from Great Yarmouth in 1970; it is seen on 5 June 1975. The depot was still standing and in use for industrial purposes in 2019.

The South Notts Bus Company commenced operations in March 1926 and established a garage in Leake Road in the village of Gotham, some 6.5 miles south of Nottingham. The company was acquired by Nottingham City Transport on 13 March 1991 and the garage was still in use by NCT as an outstation in 2019. On Sunday 20 November 1983 former Southend Transport Daimler Fleetlines WJN 352/3J were parked at the front of the garage.

OK Motor Services was based in Bishop Auckland and operated out of a garage in North Bondgate. The company was formed in the 1930s. Later renamed OK Travel, it was acquired by the Go-Ahead Group in March 1995. Former Southdown NCME-bodied Leyland PD3/4 FCD 286D was posed for the camera on 26 June 1982. The garage was subsequently demolished.

Lancashire United Transport grew to be the largest independent bus operator in the country. Initially operating trams and then trolleybuses, the first depot was established at Howe Bridge near Atherton in October 1902 (to the left of the picture). The extensive bus garage, behind NCME-bodied Guy Arab V No. 240, was opened in October 1928. The trams finished in 1933 while the replacement trolleybuses lasted until 1958. Closed by GM Buses on 7 February 1998 the only identifying feature in the area in 2019 was the overhead electricity power lines.

LUT had two other depots located at Swinton and Hindley, both of which were initially electric tram depots. Hindley Platt Bridge was opened on 7 February 1903 but lost its trams when the system closed in December 1933. In August 1974 the garage had an allocation of eighty-four buses. NCME-bodied Guy Arab V No. 129 and Bristol RESL No. 304 were among the buses present on 23 June 1974. The garage was closed in March 1986 and has been demolished.

Berresford Motors of Cheddleton was founded by James Matthew Berresford in February 1923. The original depot was in Randles Lane in Wetley Rocks, but this was soon superceded by the Cheadle Road premises. Berresfords later acquired Byrne Brothers of Leek and Stonier of Goldenhill, both of which were run as subsidiaries. Two further small operators were taken over in the 1970s. The family run concern ceased to operate the bus side of the business in September 1987 following the death of Jim Berresford. In 1968/70 twenty-six redundant Leyland PD2/1s were bought from Stockport Corporation. The former Nos 287/90 are seen in Berresfords' graveyard field on 28 February 1982. Latterly used as a trailer park there are now outdoor sports facilities on what was the garage site.

Stevensons of Uttoxeter was founded in 1926 and a depot was established in the nearby village of Spath. It remained a moderately sized operator until a merger with East Staffordshire DC Transport took place on 1 October 1985. Two years later the company took a share in Midland Fox and acquired the Swadlincote garage. In 1992 the company passed to Rhonda Buses who were bought out by Stagecoach in November 1993. In 2019 the business was part of the Arriva Group and the garage complex (still intact) was owned by a tyre and motor services company. Former London Daimler Fleetline No. DMS314 was a recent acquisition on 14 September 1979.

Camms of Nottingham originally operated out of a small depot in Faraday Road in the Lenton district of the city but in this 10 November 1979 view a number of former Ribble Motors' Leyland Leopards have spilled out on to the surrounding streets. Following deregulation Camms set up competing services in various parts of the East Midlands. The company was acquired by Dunn Line in 1999 and renamed The Nottingham Coach Company. New housing has since been built on these derelict plots and the garage is no more.

Eagre of Morton near Gainsborough was a long-established bus and coach operator. The garage was situated in Crooked Billet Street. Alongside the garage building on 26 July 1998 were former Ipswich Buses Dennis Falcons KAZ 3253/4, originally registered YDX 103/5V, and Scottish Omnibus' Leyland National RFS 582V. The stage services were sold to RoadCar in December 2001, but the coach side of the business was then registered as a separate company. This was then acquired by the Wilfreda Beehive Group of Adwick-le-Street in 2006. Although coaches are no longer kept at the site the attached booking office was still in use in 2019.

J. Fishwick & Sons two-tone green buses were a familiar sight in Leyland and Preston for well over a century. Founded in 1907, the bus side of the business operated out of garage premises in Golden Hill Lane in Leyland from the late 1930s until the company ceased trading on 24 October 2015. The buses and depot premises were subsequently sold off and the garage buildings have since assumed other uses. On 7 November 2012 Wright-bodied DAFs Nos 10 and 39 are seen parked up in the garage access road (Tuer Street).

Hulley's of Baslow first started running buses in 1921 and the following year a garage was built in Calver Road. The company was taken over by Silver Service of nearby Darley Dale in 1978 but continued to be run as a subsidiary. Silver Service sold on the former Hulley's business ten years later and it was re-registered as Hulley's of Baslow by the new owners and has continued in operation from the same base ever since. Former Burnley & Pendle Bristol RESLs LHG 385/91H were to be found at the side of the garage building on 18 September 1983. They were scrapped in 1985/4 respectively. The house in the background is also part of the depot complex.

A view of the yard at the rear of Harrow Weald garage on 24 August 1974 captures a mixture of stored and route 140 buses. The garage in the leafy High Road was opened in April 1930. The building was extended in 1933 while the yard was enlarged in 1970. HD has had a near eighty-five-year association with route 140 (operated by Hounslow from 1990–9); the RTs were replaced by Routemasters in July 1978. On view in this picture (from the left) are Nos RT3382, 2169, 4559/182, 3016, 4282/313 and 3036. The garage was operated by Metroline in 2019.

Thornton Heath bus garage was partially built on the site which was first occupied by the Croydon Tramways Company's horse tram depot, which was opened in 1879. In September 1901 a new electric tram depot was opened which in turn was replaced by the present bus garage in April 1951. Three AEC Swifts, Nos SMS246, 309 and 317, are seen at the Whitehall Road entrance on 3 September 1977. The garage was in use by Arriva London in 2019.

A new garage was opened in Church Hill in Loughton, the north-eastern extremity of the metropolis, on 2 December 1953 to cater for a predicted post-war expansion of bus services in the area. Designed to accommodate 130 buses, the allocation throughout its existence rarely exceeded fifty. It was closed on 23 May 1986. Daimler Fleetlines Nos DMS1553 and 2019 were photographed in the expanse of the garage on 29 January 1977.

Another garage which had its origins in the tramway era was at Greengate Street in West Ham. Opened by West Ham Corporation Tramways on 25 October 1906, it was originally designed to accommodate ninety tramcars. Between 1937 and 1960 it also played host to trolleybuses, during which time the capacity of the garage was not far off doubled. Closure came in October 1992 and the site has since been redeveloped with new housing and a park. One of the new roads has been given the name Routemaster Close. AEC Swifts Nos SMS622/60 were part of the garage allocation for routes S1, S3 and 238 and are seen on 26 June 1976.

In this view, captured on 29 May 1976, AEC Regal IV No. RF492 is actually parked in the bus station at Kingston. The garage was the building at the back where the RT can be seen. Kingston garage was opened on 4 January 1922, while the bus station opened six years later, and was where the last RF's bowed out on 30 April 1979. Closed in 1984 it was reopened as a minibus base in 1987. It finally closed its doors on 17 May 2000 and the site is now occupied by the Rotunda Centre.

Kingston bus garage was somewhat cramped and consequently around half of the allocation was parked up by arrangement in the railway coal yard, across the road from the garage. On 29 October 1979 a number of derelict Scania Metropolitans were to be found in the gloom with No. MD119 sandwiched between other members of the class. This site is now occupied by a new bus station which was opened on 15 July 1995.

In this 2 June 1978 view two Scanias can actually be seen in working order at Peckham garage. Also on view are consecutively numbered Routemasters Nos RM1372/3. In connection with the tramway replacement programme Peckham was opened on 2 May 1951 to replace the nearby Rye Lane tram depot. The site had previously been used by Thomas Tilling and was known as Bull Yard, which could be traced back to 1876. The garage was closed in 1994 and the site has subsequently been redeveloped with the inclusion of a new bus station.

AEC Swift No. SMS807, which was new in January 1972, is seen resting outside Romford North Street garage on 11 February 1978. Opened on 12 August 1953 the rustic brick construction was typical of a number of London Transport garages that were opened or rebuilt in the immediate post-war era. Romford was built to relieve the nearby overcrowded Hornchurch garage. It was still in use in 2019 by Stagecoach in London.

More Swifts can be seen at Potters Bar garage on 4 June 1977. In fact, Nos SMS680, 172, 677 and 684 formed two thirds of the allocation of the type as they were only scheduled to operate the 299. Potters Bar was opened in May 1930 and was located at the northern extremity of the LTE red operating area. In 1973 it played host to Routemaster FRM1, which was allocated to the 284 town service. In 2019 it was part of the Metroline group of garages.

RM1324, which is seen on 21 February 1981, was part of Southall garage's twenty-plus allocation of Routemasters for the 105 service which ran between Shepherds Bush and Heathrow Airport. Southall garage was originally known as Hanwell and was opened by the LGOC in March 1925. It was renamed in 1950 following the opening of a new Hanwell garage to the east, further along the Uxbridge Road. It suffered a disastrous fire on Christmas Day in 1985 and was subsequently closed on 8 August 1986.

Bexleyheath was opened as a new trolleybus depot on 10 November 1935. Leyland Titan No. L732 stands at the front while a row of Fleetlines wait for their next duties. The garage was an early victim of deregulation and was closed on 16 August 1986. However, it reopened in January 1988 as the base for the low-cost unit Bexleybus, which then ceased trading three years later. It then passed to London Central and eventually to Go-Ahead London.

Stockwell bus garage was opened on 6 April 1952 and has an unusual concrete arch roof structure. It was designed by Adie, Button & Partners to accommodate 200 buses and there are no internal supports. The building was Grade II listed in 1988. The first of the Routemasters specially painted for the Queen's Silver Jubilee, No. SRM1 (RM1898), is pictured under the arches on 10 April 1977. In 2019 it was operated by Go-Ahead London.

Bromley garage, in south London, was opened by the LGOC in April 1924. It was designed to accommodate sixty buses. In November 1976 the allocation was ninety vehicles. With the garage full it was often necessary to park buses in the adjacent Lower Gravel Road. With parking lights illuminated, Nos RT397, RM200, RT1560 and RM2021 are seen early on Sunday morning of 30 January 1977. To relieve the situation an open parking ground was constructed opposite in the early 1980s. The garage was still in use by Stagecoach in 2019.

At the time this picture was taken of Regal IV No. RF345, on 4 December 1976, LT's relatively small garage at Uxbridge was out on the Oxford Road. Consequently, a number of buses were parked in an open yard adjacent to Uxbridge tube station. This site was redeveloped in the early 1980s and a new bus garage was opened on 30 November 1983. Metroline was the main provider of bus services in the area in 2019.

Catford bus garage was opened by the LGOC in 1914 but was almost immediately requisitioned by the War Office. It was reopened as an operational garage in 1920. Extensive modernisation work was carried out in 1970. Later in the decade an adjacent car dealership was acquired, which is where RTs Nos 4177, 1170, 2449 and 3254 were photographed on 9 April 1977. The building behind the buses was later demolished and the original garage premises were extended. It was in use by Stagecoach in 2019.

The original Edgware bus garage, at the side of the tube station, was opened by the LGOC in April 1925. In January 1939 it was superceded by a new garage which was built on adjacent land. Modernisation was undertaken in the 1960s. Depicted in front of the main building on 19 November 1977 are Bristol LHs Nos BL76/3/2. A third structure was subsequently built further back from the main road and was opened in September 1984, replacing the building seen in the picture. The garage has been shared by London Sovereign and Metroline since 2000.

Walworth (Camberwell) electric tram depot, which was opened in 1905, had an access alongside the railway in Camberwell New Road. A new bus garage was opened by the LGOC on the opposite side of the road in 1919 with an access in Warner Road. This was later extended with an open parking yard which was built on adjacent war-damaged land. RM Nos 2215, 104 and 2199 stand in the Warner Road entrance on 10 October 1976. The garage was still in use by Go-Ahead London in 2019 although the main entrance was by then in Camberwell Station Road.

London Transport's first new garage for some time was opened at Ash Grove on 25 April 1981 to replace Dalston and Hackney garages. An OS map for the area dated 1914 shows the site to have been occupied by terraced housing and an 'Industrial School for Girls'. This view of the garage yard was taken a few days after opening, on 5 May, and depicts an array of Leyland Nationals, which at the time were deployed on the central London Red Arrow routes. This was an Arriva garage in 2019.

Above and below: The first depot to be opened in Leyton was that of the Leyton Urban District Tramways which was built on the site of a former horse tram depot in Lea Bridge Road and opened in 1905. Following the demise of the trams in 1939 it was used for trolleybuses which ran until April 1959, when the depot was closed. The staff were transferred to Leyton and Clapton bus garages. Leyton bus garage was opened by the LGOC in 1912 and was built on the site of Leyton House, opposite what was referred to as Leyton Green. The garage was badly damaged during the Second World War and wasn't fully rebuilt until the late 1950s, when it was enlarged and the capacity was increased to over 150 vehicles. It was the first garage to receive an allocation of the new RT Regent type buses in 1947. Following privatisation, the garage was briefly under the ownership of the ill-fated London Forest operator before control passed to East London and finally Stagecoach. Two contrasting views depict RM1111 on 4 June 1977 (above) and TfL Routemasters Nos LT373/85 with ADL Enviro400 Hybrid No. 12137 on 19 September 2015 (below).

Above and below: London Transport's Barking garage, in East London, has its place in history as the last garage to operate the RT Regents. The picture above depicts RT624 entering the garage as a revenue-earning bus for the last time on 7 April 1979. Situated in Longbridge Road the garage was opened in January 1924 and has played its part in maintaining London buses for not far short of a century as it was still in use by Stagecoach in 2019. It was enlarged in 1931 and has an extensive open yard on the east side. In the picture below Regent IIIs Nos RT2773, 2293 and 2816 are seen inside the garage on 2 September 1978, resting between duties.

Palmers Green garage was opened by the LGOC in July 1912 and has been going strong ever since. It was modernised during the 1970s and gained an open parking yard in 2016 when two adjacent properties were demolished. Leyland Fleetline No. DMS2444 is seen departing the now Arriva-owned garage on 11 March 1978.

Stonebridge Park was one of forty or so electric tram depots which were built in the capital. It was originally constructed for the Metropolitan Electric Tramways Company and was opened on 10 October 1906. In 1936 it was extended to accommodate trolleybuses which operated from the depot until January 1962. Seen inside on 27 May 1978 are Nos RM2177 and DMS1973, flanking preserved Leyland No. RTL453. The garage was closed on 15 August 1981 but was still in use in 2019 for industrial purposes.

Western SMT's area of operation stretched from the outskirts of Glasgow all the way south to Carlisle, where the operator opened a garage in Lonsdale Street in 1935. Sub-depots existed at Langholm and Longtown. The garage was closed in 1981 with most of the buildings being demolished to create additional parking space for the adjacent Lowther Street bus station. Alexander-bodied Bristol MW No. 1594 of Dumfries depot is about to depart on 26 May 1976.

On 9 January 1982 Eastern Scottish (Scottish Omnibuses) Plaxton-bodied Seddon Pennine No. YS955 had taken refuge in Ribble's Carlisle Willowholme garage. Ribble moved their operations from the Corporation Road garage to a new garage at Willowholme on 2 November 1968. The company was acquired by Stagecoach on 21 April 1989 and the garage was still in use in 2019.

Right and below: Edinburgh Corporation's (now Lothian Buses) Central bus garage was opened in 1926 and has a capacity for around 240 buses. It has a prominent glass dome on the roof, which can be seen in the lower picture. In this August 2014 view Volvo B7TL No. 806 and Dennis Trident No. 624 are seen at rest. In 2019 a fleet of seventy-eight new tri-axle Volvo B8Ls was part of the garage's extensive allocation.

Longstone garage, in the west of the city, was built on the former Hailes Brickworks site and was opened in 1955 and initially replaced Gorgie tram depot and later Tollcross (a former tram depot) bus garage. The garage has an extensive open parking yard and a new maintenance building was opened in 2013. On view in this March 2015 view are Lothian Buses Nos 417, 727, 991, 665, 917, 725, 116 and Training Bus TB51.

The third of Lothian's city bus garages is situated on the south bank of the Firth of Forth. Opened in 1962 it was built on the site of the Marine Pleasure Gardens and consequently is known as Marine garage. On 23 April 1976 one of the last of the tramway replacement MCCW-bodied Leyland PD2/20s, No. 741, was photographed adjacent to the maintenance building. The garage was later extended to accommodate the large fleet of sight-seeing tour buses.

More than forty years later the garage had not changed that much, although the extension can be seen on the right. The garage has a capacity to accommodate more than 200 buses. Lothian's last Dennis Tridents were taken out of service in 2019 but Nos 628/29/61/41/60/59/49 had already been retired when this picture was taken on 22 June 2018. Lothian Buses was still owned by Edinburgh, East and West Lothian councils at the time. A separate works facility existed a short distance away, along Seafield Road.

Lothian Buses acquired the former Scottish Omnibuses/Eastern Scottish Mall Avenue bus garage in Musselburgh when it was taken over from FirstBus (formerly the GRT Bus Group) in August 2016. In 2019 it was in use by Lothian's East Coast Buses' subsidiary company, whose livery is carried by former Lothian Trident No. (20)614 in this 23 August 2016 view. Also seen are Trident No. (20)626 and Volvo B9TL No. 20942, which is painted in what became Lothian's Country bus livery. ECB is now firmly established in the area with services in East Lothian and to Edinburgh.

AA (Ayr-Ardrossan) Motor Services was formed in 1930 and latterly had just two constituent operators – Youngs of Ayr and Dodds of Troon (founded in 1910). The latter had a garage base in Dundonald Road. This venerable line-up was photographed in the garage yard on Saturday 27 March 1976 and comprised Bristol KSW SRB 542, AEC Regent III OKM 317 and Guy Arabs PUF 631, GSD 779 and TSD 630. While the stage carriage side of the business was acquired by Stagecoach in 1997, the coach business, which was run separately, was still going strong in 2019 and was based in Ayr. The site of the Troon premises has been redeveloped.

The A1 Service consortium of operators was formed in May 1931 and ran bus services in Ayrshire and each operator had their own buses and garage, although a common fleet livery was adopted. This is a view of the parking lot adjacent to Ian Duff's garage in Parkhouse Road in Ardrossan. Featured on 12 April 1978 are three Atlanteans with contrasting bodywork, belonging to James McKinnon (JSD 941F), Andrew Hunter (KSD 661F) and Claude Dunn (WCS 830K). A1 was acquired by Stagecoach in January 1995 and the garage site was subsequently occupied by a petrol filling station and a car dealership.

Each of the A1 operators owned only single-figure numbers of buses and the garages were often quite small. Daimler CVG6 TCS 103 was purchased by James Brown, whose garage was in Townfoot, in Dreghorn, in February 1962. It was captured under cover on 1 June 1976. The Daimler was withdrawn two years later and there is now a new housing development known as Townfoot Lane on the site of the garage. Andrew Hunter also had a garage in Dreghorn.

There were a number of small independent operators in the Paisley area of which Cunningham's Bus Services was one. The garage was located in a former coal depot yard next to the railway in Underwood Road. Former Ribble Burlingham-bodied Leyland PD3/4 KCK 910 (No. 1549) and Yorkshire Traction NCME-bodied Leyland PD3A/1 VHE 200 (No. 1200) were present on 12 April 1978. Cunningham's was acquired by Western SMT in 1979.

Another Paisley operator was Graham's Bus Service Ltd whose garage was located opposite the cemetery in Hawkhead Road, another collector of second-hand buses. Ex-Tent Roe-bodied Atlantean TCH 93 is seen alongside newly purchased Daimler CRG HXS 864 in the garage yard on 12 April 1978. Having been founded in the 1920s, the operator ceased trading on 29 April 1990. There was no trace of the garage in 2019 with the land an open expanse.

Dundee Corporation originally had two tram depots, which were opened in the early 1900s, both of which later housed motorbuses. Lochee depot was closed when the more central and larger East Dock Street bus garage was opened in the mid-1950s; it consisted of a large open parking ground and a maintenance building. A row of Daimler CVGs is pictured on 15 May 1977. The blue and white Tayside colours had superceded the Dundee green. The garage was still in use by Tayside's successor National Express in 2019, while Maryfield garage had long since closed.

Aberdeen Corporation Tramways operated out of six depots. King Street depot was built on part of the Parade Ground of an Army Barracks (The Royal Aberdeenshire Highlanders Regiment) and was opened in 1914, but was then requisitioned by the War Department, eventually functioning as a tram depot in 1919. It was extended in 1932, with the acquisition of the adjacent Advocates Park Football Ground, to accommodate both buses and trams. The last trams ran in May 1958 and King Street was further extended to accommodate the entire bus fleet, mostly out in the open. Some nineteen Alexander-bodied Grampian Atlanteans can be seen in this view taken on 26 March 1983. Following acquisitions, the GRT Group was formed which became FirstBus after the merger with Badgerline in April 1995. A new depot was opened on the same site on 15 July 2010 which was firmly established as the First Group head office.

The Alexander Bus Company was split into three separate operating units in 1961, one of which was the yellow and cream painted buses of Alexander Northern. The Aberdeen garage was located in Gairn Terrace and is where Leyland PD3A/3 No. RB284 was photographed on 31 May 1975. The operator was renamed Northern Scottish in June 1985 and later acquired by Stagecoach in March 1991. The garage has since been demolished and the site redeveloped.

Highland Omnibuses was formed in 1952 with the amalgamation of Highland Transport, Macrae & Dick and Alexanders Town Services of Inverness. The newly created operating area was very extensive and included road transport on some of the larger northern isles. Former MacBrayne Duple-bodied Bedford VAS No. CD43 was caught resting opposite the Park Road garage in Portree, on the Isle of Skye, on 17 May 1975. The, by then fragmented, company was acquired by Stagecoach on 16 May 2008 but the garage remained in use until August 2016 when a new depot was opened in Broom Place.

When this former Central SMT Bristol FLF HGM 334E was photographed at the Stagecoach garage in Perth, on 20 April 1985, little did anyone know (except perhaps Brian Souter and his sister Ann Gloag) that Stagecoach would grow to become the largest bus operator in the UK. First established in 1980 the company grew steadily in the early 1980s before expanding at a rapid rate after deregulation. The group head office was still based in Perth in 2019.

Tom Alexander acquired the Hunter & Nelson Coach Operator of Arbroath in 1961 and commenced trading as Greyhound Luxury Coaches. Garage premises were established in Airlie Crescent. The fleet mainly comprised second-hand acquisitions, as evidenced by this view of former Chesterfield Corporation Leyland PD2A 66 SRB, which could be seen in the yard on 10 September 1977. Tom Alexander died in 1980 and the business was sold to Tayside Regional Transport ten years later. In 2019 there was no trace left of the garage or Airlie Crescent.

The London Transport Museum in Covent Garden was opened in 1980 and is laid out in a Victorian iron and glass building which was a former market and dates from 1871. The exhibits on view in this September 1995 view are AECs Nos NS1995 of 1926, LT165 of 1930 and RT4825 of 1954 along with Leyland K2 Trolleybus No. 1253 of 1939.

The Black Country Living Museum in Dudley Road, in Tipton, was opened in 1979. Here the visitor can avail themselves of a ride on a vintage bus, tram and trolleybus. Seen receiving attention in a modern equipped workshop, on 21 May 2016, is preserved West Bromwich Corporation 1929 Dixon-bodied Dennis E Type No. 32. The motorbus collection also included a former West Bromwich 1948 Daimler, a Midland Red BMMO D9 and a 1948 Guy Vixen.

London Transport's Fulwell garage was opened as an electric tramcar depot for the London United Tramways in 1902. In June 1931 it was the first London depot to host trolleybuses. Long after the trams and trolleybuses had departed, on 5 December 1976, preserved lowbridge AEC Regent III No. RLH23 and Leyland No. RTW467 were to be found tucked away in a corner. Such was the expanse of Fulwell that it was shared by Abellio London and London United in 2019.

In 2019 the Sandtoft Trolleybus Museum, near Doncaster, celebrated fifty years of operation. When it was opened in 1969 there were just four systems still operating in the UK, with the last in Bradford finishing on 26 March 1972. With some sixty preserved trolleybuses on site, around twenty different UK operators are represented. Bradford No. 746 is an English Electric-bodied BUT9611T which dates from 1949.

Opened in the late 1930s, the former Brighton Hove & District's Whitehawk garage in Brighton was playing host to an unusual mix of buses on 4 May 1980. Taking refuge are preserved Bamber Bridge Motor Services ELC-bodied AEC Regent III No. 4, London Country Roe-bodied Atlantean No. AN222 and Croydon garage's recently overhauled AEC Routemaster No. RM812. The occasion was the annual Historic Commercial Vehicle Society Rally. The garage was still in use by Go-Ahead in 2019.

Some garages live to fight another day. The former Hall Street depot in St Helens was reopened (for the second time) as the Northwest Museum of Transport in 1991 and has become home to a diverse range of preserved buses. Former Darwen Corporation ELC-bodied Crossley-badged AEC Regent V No. 17 was among the residents on 10 September 2006. Leyland manufactured buses from Warrington and Preston Corporations can be seen on either side.

The Museum of Transport in Manchester occupies the two former Manchester Corporation bus garage buildings which were tacked on to Queens Road tram depot in 1928 and 1935. Opened on 4 May 1979 the exhibits are mainly drawn from the Lancashire bus fleets which could be seen in the Manchester conurbation. Stockport and Manchester Corporation Crossleys No. 321 of 1951 and No. 2150 of 1948 are prominent in this December 2010 view.

The last picture features not an operational garage but a final resting place for buses. Between 1965 and 2005 Wombwell Diesels dealt with numerous redundant London buses as they were systematically scrapped. This view of former LTE RT Regents, seen on 23 May 1978, was typical of the scene that greeted the occasional visitor. Some of these buses had still been in service just a few weeks previously. A new residential housing estate now occupies this site.